The ESSENTIALS® of

DIFFERENTIAL EQUATIONS I

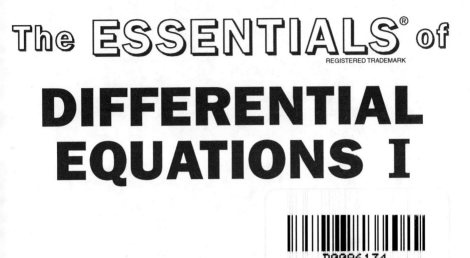

D0096134

Staff of Research and Education Association, Dr. M. Fogiel, Director

> This book covers the usual course outline of Differential Equations I. For more advanced topics, see *"THE ESSENTIALS OF DIFFERENTIAL EQUATIONS II."*

Research & Education Association
61 Ethel Road West
Piscataway, New Jersey 08854

THE ESSENTIALS®
OF DIFFERENTIAL EQUATIONS I

Printed in the United States of America

Library of Congress Catalog Card Number 98-66019

International Standard Book Number 0-87891-581-8

WHAT "THE ESSENTIALS" WILL DO FOR YOU

This book is a review and study guide. It is comprehensive and it is concise.

It helps in preparing for exams, in doing homework, and remains a handy reference source at all times.

It condenses the vast amount of detail characteristic of the subject matter and summarizes the **essentials** of the field.

It will thus save hours of study and preparation time.

The book provides quick access to the important facts, principles, theorems, concepts, and equations of the field.

Materials needed for exams, can be reviewed in summary form — eliminating the need to read and re-read many pages of textbook and class notes. The summaries will even tend to bring detail to mind that had been previously read or noted.

This "ESSENTIALS" book has been carefully prepared by educators and professionals and was subsequently reviewed by another group of editors to assure accuracy and maximum usefulness.

Dr. Max Fogiel
Program Director

CONTENTS

CONTENTS

CHAPTER 1

BASIC DEFINITIONS AND CLASSIFICATIONS

1. A differential equation is an equation which involves derivatives of an unknown function.

2. An ordinary differential equation is an equation which involves only ordinary derivatives.

3. A partial differential equation is an equation which involves partial derivatives.

4. The order of a differential equation is the order of the highest derivative that appears in the equation.

5. The degree of a differential equation is the greatest exponent of the highest ordered derivative in the equation.

6. A linear ordinary differential equation has the general form

$$a_0(x)\frac{d^n y}{dx^n} + a_1(x)\frac{d^{n-1} y}{dx^{n-1}} + \ldots + a_{n-1}(x)\frac{dy}{dx} + a_n(x)y = b(x),$$

where a_0 is not identically zero.

The conditions for a linear equation are:

a) The dependent variable and its derivatives occur only in the first degree.

b) No product of the dependent variable and/or any of its derivatives are present.

c) No transcendental function of the dependent variable and/or its derivatives occur.

7. The question of existence: Does an equation have a solution or not?

8. The question of uniqueness: Given an equation with a solution, does it have other solutions? If so, what type of additional conditions must be specified to single out a particular solution?

9. The general solution (or primitive) of a differential equation is a relation between the variables which involves n arbitrary constants.

10. The constants in the general solution are called essential if they cannot be replaced by a smaller number of constants.

11. The primitive is the equation of a family of curves called integral curves. A particular solution is obtained from the primitive by assigning definite values to the arbitrary constants, and is identified as one of the integral curves.

12. A primitive involving n essential arbitrary constants will give rise to a differential equation of order n with no arbitrary constants. This equation is obtained when you eliminate the n constants by differentiating the primitive n times with respect to the independent variable.

CHAPTER 2

FIRST ORDER EQUATIONS

2.1 LINEAR EQUATIONS

Given a first-order, ordinary linear equation of the general form

$$\frac{dy}{dx} + P(x)y = Q(x) \tag{2.1}$$

multiply both sides by an integrating factor

$$u(x) = e^{\int^x P(x)dx} \tag{2.2}$$

to get

$$\frac{d}{dx}(u(x)y) = u(x)Q(x).$$

The general solution for (2.1) is then

$$y = \frac{1}{u(x)} \int u(x)Q(x)dx + c \tag{2.3}$$

Simple solutions:

1. For $\frac{dy}{dx} = f(x)$,

$$\boxed{y = \int f(x)\,dx + c}$$

2. For $\dfrac{dy}{dx} + ay = 0$ where a = constant,

$$\boxed{y = ce^{-ax}}$$

3. For $\dfrac{dy}{dx} + ay = g(x)$,

$$\boxed{y = e^{-ax} \int e^{ax}g(x)\,dx + ce^{-ax}}$$

2.2 SEPARABLE EQUATIONS

If an equation of the form

$$M(x,y) + N(x,y)\,\frac{dy}{dx} = 0$$

can be written

$$\boxed{M(x)M(y)\,dx + N(x)N(y)\,dy = 0} \tag{2.4}$$

it is said to be separable.

Separating the variables gives

$$\frac{M(x)}{N(x)}\,dx + \frac{N(y)}{M(y)}\,dy = 0.$$

The general solution for (2.4) is

4

$$\int^{x} \frac{M(x)}{N(x)} \, dx + \int^{y} \frac{N(y)}{M(y)} \, dy = c \qquad (2.5)$$

2.3 EXACT EQUATIONS

An exact equation has the form

$$M(x,y) + N(x,y) \frac{dy}{dx} = 0 \; ,$$

where $\qquad\qquad\qquad\qquad\qquad$ (2.6)

$$\frac{\partial M}{\partial y} = \frac{\partial N}{\partial x}$$

When an equation is exact there exists a function $\mu(x,y)$ such that

$$\frac{\partial \mu(x,y)}{\partial x} = M(x,y) \quad \text{and} \quad \frac{\partial \mu(x,y)}{\partial y} = N(x,y)$$

for all $(x,y) \in D$.

Hence the equation may be written

$$\frac{\partial \mu(x,y)}{\partial x} \, dx + \frac{\partial \mu(x,y)}{\partial y} \, dy = 0 \; ,$$

and $\mu(x,y)$ may be determined.

Solution:

1. Find $\mu(x,y)$:

$$\mu(x,y) = \int M(x,y) dx + \phi(y) \qquad (2.7)$$

(Holding y as a constant.)

2. Set $\frac{\partial \mu}{\partial y} = N(x,y)$, Holding x as a constant.

3. Solve for $\phi'(y)$:

$$\phi'(y) = N(x,y) - \int \frac{\partial M(x,y)dx}{\partial y} \qquad (2.8)$$

4. Substituting back into (2.7) gives the general solution

$$\boxed{\begin{array}{l} \mu(x,y) = \int M(x,y)dx + \int \phi'(y)dx \\[2mm] \text{where } \phi'(y) \text{ is given by } (2.8) \end{array}} \qquad (2.9)$$

2.4 INTEGRATING FACTORS

If the equation

$$M(x,y)dx + N(x,y)dy = 0 \qquad (2.10)$$

is not exact, then an integrating factor is sought to make (2.10) exact.

1. If $\dfrac{\frac{\partial M}{\partial y} - \frac{\partial N}{\partial x}}{N}$ is a function of x alone, then

$$\boxed{\mu(x) = \exp\left[\int \frac{\frac{\partial M}{\partial y} - \frac{\partial N}{\partial x}}{N} dx\right]} \qquad (2.11)$$

is the integrating factor of (2.10).

2. If $\dfrac{\frac{\partial M}{\partial y} - \frac{\partial N}{\partial x}}{-M}$ is a function of y alone, then

$$\mu(y) = \exp\left[\int \frac{\frac{\partial M}{\partial y} - \frac{\partial N}{\partial x}}{-M}\, dy\right] \tag{2.12}$$

is the integrating factor of (2.10).

3. If $\frac{\partial M}{\partial x} + \frac{\partial N}{\partial y} \neq 0$, then

$$\mu(x,y) = \frac{1}{\frac{\partial M}{\partial x} + \frac{\partial N}{\partial y}} \tag{2.13}$$

is the integrating factor of (2.10).

4. If (2.10) can be written in the form

$$yf(x,y)dx + xg(x,y)dy = 0, \tag{2.14}$$

where

$$f(x,y) \neq g(x,y),$$

then

$$\mu(x,y) = \frac{1}{\frac{\partial M}{\partial x} - \frac{\partial N}{\partial y}} \tag{2.15}$$

is the integrating factor of (2.14).

For an equation of the form

$$x^r y^s (mydx + nxdy) + x^\rho y^\sigma (\mu ydx + \nu xdy) = 0 \tag{2.16}$$

where r, s, m, n, ρ, σ, μ, ν are constants and $m\nu - n\mu \neq 0$, an integrating factor exists of the form

$$\boxed{x^{\alpha} y^{\beta} = \mu(x,y)} \qquad (2.17)$$

where α and β are determined by substituting (2.17) into (2.16).

Sometimes an integrating factor may be found by inspection, after grouping the terms in the equation, and recognizing a certain group as being a part of an exact differential. For example:

Group of Terms	Intergrating Factor	Exact Differential
x dy - y dx	$\dfrac{1}{x^2}$	$\dfrac{xdy - ydx}{x^2} = d\left(\dfrac{y}{x}\right)$
x dy - y dx	$\dfrac{1}{y^2}$	$-\dfrac{ydx - xdy}{y^2} = d\left(-\dfrac{x}{y}\right)$
x dy - y dx	$\dfrac{1}{xy}$	$\dfrac{dy}{y} - \dfrac{dx}{x} = d(\ln \dfrac{y}{x})$
x dy - y dx	$\dfrac{1}{x^2 + y^2}$	$\dfrac{xdy - ydx}{x^2 + y^2} = \dfrac{\frac{xdy - ydx}{x^2}}{1 + (\frac{y}{x})^2}$ $= d(\text{arc}\tan\dfrac{y}{x})$
xdy + ydx	$\dfrac{1}{(xy)^n}$	$\dfrac{xdy + ydx}{(xy)^n} = d\{\dfrac{-1}{(n-1)(xy)^{n-1}}\}$ if $n \neq 1$
		$\dfrac{xdy + ydx}{xy} = d\{\ln(xy)\}$, if $n = 1$
xdx + ydy	$\dfrac{1}{(x^2+y^2)^n}$	$\dfrac{xdx + ydy}{(x^2+y^2)^n}$ $= d\{\dfrac{-1}{2(n-1)(x^2+y^2)^{n-1}}\}$ if $n \neq 1$

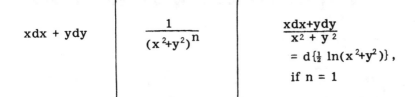

$x\,dx + y\,dy$	$\dfrac{1}{(x^2+y^2)^n}$	$\dfrac{x\,dx+y\,dy}{x^2+y^2}$ $= d\{\tfrac{1}{2}\ln(x^2+y^2)\}\,,$ if $n = 1$

2.5 HOMOGENEOUS EQUATIONS

If the equation

$$\frac{dy}{dx} = f(x,y) \qquad (2.18)$$

depends only on the ratio $\dfrac{y}{x}$ or $\dfrac{x}{y}$, then it is said to be Homogeneous.

Let $\qquad y = vx$

and $\qquad \dfrac{dy}{dx} = x\,\dfrac{dv}{dx} + v,$

Then (2.18) becomes

$$\boxed{\; x\,\frac{dv}{dx} + v = F(v) \;} \qquad (2.19)$$

a separable equation, which can be solved by direct integration. After solving, replace v by $\dfrac{y}{x}$ to get the solution to (2.18).

A function $f(x,y)$ is called Homogeneous of degree n if

$$\boxed{\; f(\lambda x, \lambda y) = \lambda^n f(x,y) \;} \qquad (2.20)$$

9

2.6 NON-HOMOGENEOUS EQUATIONS

Consider the equation

$$(a_1x+b_1y+c_1)dx + (a_2x+b_2y+c_2)dy = 0 \qquad (2.21)$$

where $a_1, b_1, c_1, a_2, b_2, c_2$ are all constants.

1. If $a_1b_2 - a_2b_1 = 0$, use the transformation

$$t = a_1x + b_1y,$$
$$dy = \frac{dt - a_1dx}{b_1} \qquad (2.22)$$

to reduce (2.21) to a separable form:

$$P(x,t)dx + Q(x,t)dt = 0 \qquad (2.23)$$

2. If $a_1b_2 - b_1a_2 \neq 0$, use the transformation

$$x = X + h,$$
$$y = Y + k \qquad (2.24)$$

where h and k are solutions of the system

$$a_1h + b_1k + c_1 = 0,$$
$$a_2h + b_2k + c_2 = 0 \qquad (2.25)$$

to reduce (2.21) to the Homogeneous Equation

$$(a_1X+b_1Y)dX + (a_2X+b_2Y)dY = 0 \qquad (2.26)$$

For an equation of the form

$$yf(xy)dx + xg(xy)dy = 0 \qquad (2.27)$$

use the transformation

$$z = xy,$$
$$y = z/x, \qquad (2.28)$$
$$dy = \frac{x\,dz - z\,dx}{x^2}$$

to reduce (2.27) to a separable form:

$$P(x,z)dx + Q(x,z)dz = 0 \qquad (2.29)$$

2.7 FIRST-ORDER EQUATIONS OF HIGHER DEGREE

Consider a first-order equation of the general form

$$p^n + p_1(x,y)p^{n-1} + \ldots + P_{n-1}(x,y)p + P_n(x,y) = 0 \qquad (2.30)$$

where $p = y' = \dfrac{dy}{dx}$.

Equations Solvable for p

1. Put (2.30) into the form

    $$(p-F_1)(p-F_2)\ldots(p-Fn) = 0 \qquad (2.31)$$

    where $F = F(x,y)$.

11

2. Set each factor = 0 and solve the following resulting equations:

$$\frac{dy}{dx} = F_1(x,y), \ \frac{dy}{dx} = F_2(x,y) \ \ldots \ \frac{dy}{dx} = f_n(x,y). \qquad (2.32)$$

3. The general solution is the product of the solutions of (2.32):

$$\boxed{y = f_1(x,y,c) \cdot f_2(x,y,c)\ldots f_n(x,y,c) = 0} \qquad (2.33)$$

Equations solvable for y, consider

$$\boxed{y = f(x,p), \ p = \frac{dy}{dx}} \qquad (2.34)$$

1. Differentiate (2.34) with respect to x:

$$P = \frac{\partial f}{\partial x} + \frac{\partial f}{\partial p}\frac{dp}{dx} = F(x, \ p, \ \frac{dp}{dx}). \qquad (2.35)$$

2. Solve (2.35), an equation of first order and first degree:

$$\phi(x,p,c) = 0 \qquad (2.36)$$

3. Obtain the general solution by eliminating p between (2.34) and (2.36), or by expressing x and y separately as functions of p.

Equations Solvable for x

Consider

$$\boxed{x = f(y,p)} \qquad (2.37)$$

1. Differentiate with respect to y:

$$\frac{dx}{dy} = \frac{1}{p} = \frac{\partial f}{\partial y} + \frac{\partial f}{\partial p}\frac{dp}{dy} = F(y, \ p, \ \frac{dp}{dy}) \qquad (2.38)$$

2. Solve (2.38):

$$\phi(y,p,c) = 0 \qquad (2.39)$$

3. Obtain the general solution by eliminating p between (2.37) and (2.39), or by expressing x and y separately as functions of p.

2.8 CLAIRAUT EQUATION

Consider a Clairaut equation of the general form

$$\boxed{y = px + f(p)} \qquad (2.40)$$

where $p \equiv \dfrac{dy}{dx}$.

The general solution is obtained by replacing p by c:

$$\boxed{y = cx + f(c)} \qquad (2.41)$$

2.9 BERNOULLI DIFFERENTIAL EQUATION

Consider a Bernoulli differential equation of the general form

$$\boxed{\dfrac{dy}{dx} + P(x)y = Q(x)y^n} \qquad (2.42)$$

Solution:

13

1. Divide through by y^n:

$$y^{-n} \frac{dy}{dx} + P(x)y^{1-n} = Q(x) \qquad (2.43)$$

2. Make the substitution

$$v = y^{1-n}$$

which gives

$$\frac{dv}{dx} + P_1(x)v = Q_1(x) \qquad (2.44)$$

where $P_1(x) = (1-n)P(x),$

$Q_1(x) = (1-n)Q(x).$

3. Equation (2.44) is a first-order linear equation solvable

by using the integtrating factor $\mu(x)^2 e^{\int P_1(x)dx}$

CHAPTER 3

SECOND ORDER EQUATIONS

3.1 BASIC CONCEPTS

The problem of finding a solution for

$$\frac{d^2y}{dx^2} + P(x)\frac{dy}{dx} + Q(x)y = G(x) \tag{3.1}$$

on the interval $x_0 < x < x_1$, while satisfying the conditions

$$y(x_0) = A,$$

$$y(x_1) = B,$$

is known as a boundary value problem.

The homogeneous, or reduced, or complementary equation is

$$y'' + P(x)y' + Q(x)y = 0, \tag{3.2}$$

and is obtained from (3.1) by setting $G(x) = 0$.

3.2 FUNDAMENTAL SOLUTIONS TO HOMOGENEOUS EQUATIONS

The differential operator is defined

$$L[\phi] = \phi'' + p\phi' + q\phi$$

or

$$L = D^2 + pD + q,$$

in which D is the Derivative Operator.

1. If $y = y_1(x)$ and $y = y_2(x)$ are solutions to

$$L[y] = y'' + P(x)y' + q(x)y = 0, \qquad (3.3)$$

then

$$y = C_1 y_1(x) + C_2 y_2(x)$$

is also a solution to (3.3); C_1 and C_2 are arbitrary constants.

2. $y_1(x)$ and $y_2(x)$ are a set of fundamental solutions.

3. The wronskian is

$$W(y_1, y_2) = \begin{vmatrix} y_1 & y_2 \\ y_1' & y_2' \end{vmatrix} = y_1 y_2' - y_1' y_2. \qquad (3.4)$$

In general,

$$W(f_1, f_2, \ldots, f_n) = \begin{vmatrix} f_1 & f_2 & \cdots & f_n \\ f_1' & f_2' & \cdots & f_n' \\ \vdots & & & \\ f_1^{(n-1)} & f_2^{(n-1)} & \cdots & f_n^{(n-1)} \end{vmatrix}$$

4. $W(y_1, y_2)$ is either identically zero, or else is never zero.

3.3 LINEAR INDEPENDENCE

A set of functions $\{f_1, \ldots, f_n\}$ is said to be linearly dependent if there exists a set of constants c's not equal to zero such that

$$c_1f_1 + c_2f_2 + \ldots + c_nf_n = 0.$$

Alternatively, if $W(x,y)$ is never zero, then x and y are linearly independent.

3.4 REDUCTION OF ORDER

Consider the equation

$$y'' + p(x)y' + q(x)y = 0. \qquad (3.5)$$

If one solution,

$$y = y_1(x),$$

is known, a second solution can be determined:

$$y = y_2(x) = v(x)y_1(x). \qquad (3.6)$$

Differentiating (3.6) and substituting into (3.5) gives

$$v'' + (p + 2\frac{y_1'}{y_1})v' = 0, \qquad (3.7)$$

which is a first-order linear equation in v'.

Solving (3.7) gives

$$v' = c \exp\left[-\int p(x) + \frac{y_1'(x)}{y_1(x)}\, dx\right] = cu(x).$$

Integrating again gives

$$v = c\int u(x)dx.$$

The general solution of (3.5) is

$$y = c_1y_1(x) + c_2y_1(x) \int u(x)dx. \qquad (3.8)$$

3.5 HOMOGENEOUS EQUATIONS WITH CONSTANT COEFFICIENTS

Consider the equation

$$ay'' + by' + cy = 0 \qquad (3.9)$$

The characteristic or auxilary equation of this is

$$ar^2 + br + c = 0 \qquad (3.10)$$

The roots of (3.10) are

and

$$r_1 = \frac{-b+(b^2-4ac)^{\frac{1}{2}}}{2a}$$

$$r_2 = \frac{-b-(b^2-4ac)^{\frac{1}{2}}}{2a} \qquad (3.11)$$

1. If the roots are real and unequal ($b^2 - 4ac > 0$),

$$y = c_1e^{r_1x} + c_2e^{r_2x} \qquad (3.12)$$

2. If the roots are real and equal ($b^2 - 4ac = 0$),

$$y = c_1e^{r_1x} + c_2xe^{r_1x} \qquad (3.13)$$

3. If the roots are complex ($b^2 - 4ac < 0$),

$$y = c_1 e^{\lambda x} \cos \mu x + c_2 e^{\lambda x} \sin \mu x$$

where

$$\lambda = \frac{-b}{2a} \; ; \quad \mu = \frac{(b^2 - 4ac)^{\frac{1}{2}}}{2a}$$

(3.14)

3.6 NON-HOMOGENEOUS EQUATIONS

The solution to a homogeneous equation,

$$y'' + P(x)y' + Q(x)y = 0,$$

(3.2)

is called a complementary solution and denoted by y_c.

The solution of a non-homogeneous equation is

$$y = y_c + y_p$$

where y_p is the particular solution of the non-homogeneous equation.

Two methods of finding a particular solution are:

1. The method of undetermined coefficients

2. The method of variation of parameters.

3.7 METHOD OF UNDETERMINED COEFFICIENTS

Consider $y'' + ay' + by = f(x)$ (3.15)

1. The characteristic solution, y_c, is determined by setting $F(x) = 0$.

2. Now use $F(x)$ to determine the particular solution, y_p (compare y_1 with y_c to make sure they are not similar).

3. To find the undetermined coefficients, substitute y_p, y_p', y_p'' into the differential equation for $y_1, dy/dx$, d^2y/dx^2, respectively.

4. $y = y_c + y_p$

$f(x)$	$y_p(x)$
$a_0x^n + a_1x^{n-1} + \ldots + a_n = P_n(x)$	$x^s(A_0x^n + A_1x^{n-1} + \ldots + A_n)$
$P_n(x)e^{\alpha x}$	$x^s(A_0x^n + A_1x^{n-1} + \ldots + A_n)e^{\alpha x}$
$P_n(x)e^{\alpha x} \begin{cases} \sin \beta x \\ \cos \beta x \end{cases}$	$x^s[A_0x^n + A_1x^{n-1} + \ldots + A_n)e^{\alpha x}$ $\cos \beta x + (B_0x^n + B_1x^{n-1} + \ldots$ $+ B_n)e^{\alpha x}\sin \beta x]$

s is the smallest nonnegative integer ($s=0$, 1, or 2) to ensure that no term in $y_p(x)$ is also the solution of the corresponding homogeneous equation

3.8 METHOD OF VARIATION OF PARAMETERS

Also referred to as Lagrange's Method, this method applies in all cases (including variable coefficients) in which the complementary function is known.

Consider the equation

$$\boxed{y'' + a_1y' + a_2y = f(x)} \qquad (3.16)$$

where a_1 and a_2 are constants.

First solve the homogeneous equation $(f(x) = 0)$.

The particular solution is

$$y_p(x) = u_1y_1(x) + u_2y_2(x) \qquad (3.17)$$

where u_1 and u_2 must simultaneously satisfy

and
$$\begin{aligned} u_1'(x)y_1(x) + u_2'(x)y_2(x) &= 0 \\ u_1'(x)y_1'(x) + u_2'(x)y_2'(x) &= f(x). \end{aligned} \qquad (3.18)$$

Using Cramer's rule,

$$u_1' = \frac{\begin{vmatrix} 0 & y_2(x) \\ f(x) & y_2'(x) \end{vmatrix}}{W(y_1, y_2)}$$

and

$$u_2' = \frac{\begin{vmatrix} y_1(x) & 0 \\ y_2'(x) & f(x) \end{vmatrix}}{W(y_1, y_2)}$$

Therefore, the general solution is $\qquad (3.19)$

$$\boxed{y_p(x) = -y_1(x)\int \frac{y_2(x)f(x)}{W(y_1, y_2)}\,dx + y_2(x)\int \frac{y_1(x)f(x)}{W(y_1, y_2)}\,dx}$$

3.9 RICCATI'S EQUATION

Consider a second-order equation of the form

$$a_2(x)u'' + a_1(x)u' + a_0(x)u = 0. \qquad (3.20)$$

The corresponding Riccati's equation is

$$\frac{dy}{dx} = \frac{-a_0(x)}{f(x)a_2(x)} - \left\{\frac{a_1(x)}{a_2(x)} + \frac{f'(x)}{f(x)}\right\}y - f(x)y^2 \qquad (3.21)$$

If (3.21) can be solved as

$$y = y(x),$$

then the general solution to (3.20) is

$$u(x) = e^{\int f(x)y(x)dx} \qquad (3.22)$$

The function $f(x)$ is chosen to make (3.21) as simple as possible to solve.

3.10 LINEAR EQUATIONS WITH VARIABLE COEFFICIENTS

Consider the equation

$$\frac{d^2y}{dx^2} + R(x)\frac{dy}{dx} + S(x)y = Q(x). \qquad (3.23)$$

Let $y = u(x)v(x)$. Then (3.23) becomes

$$\frac{d^2v}{dx^2} + R_1(x)\frac{dv}{dx} + S_1(x)V = Q_1(x) \qquad (3.24)$$

where

$$R_1(x) = \frac{2}{u}\frac{du}{dx} + R(x),$$

$$S_1(x) = \frac{1}{u}\left\{\frac{d^2u}{dx^2} + R(x)\frac{du}{dx} + S(x)u\right\}$$

22

and

$$Q_1(x) = \frac{Q(x)}{u}.$$

u(x) is chosen so that $R_1(x) = \frac{2}{u} \frac{du}{dx} + R(x) = 0$

or $\quad \frac{du}{u} = -\tfrac{1}{2}R(x).$

Then

$$u(x) = e^{-\frac{1}{2} \int R(x)\,dx}$$

$$S_1(x) = S(x) - \tfrac{1}{4}R(x)^2 - \tfrac{1}{2}\frac{dR(x)}{dx}$$

and

$$Q_1(x) = \frac{Q(x)}{u}.$$

1. If $S_1(x) = A$, where A = constant, then (3.24) becomes

$$\boxed{\frac{d^2v}{dx^2} + AV = \frac{Q(x)}{u(x)}} \qquad (3.25)$$

   a linear equation with constant coefficients.

2. If $S_1(x) = \frac{A}{x^2}$, Then (3.24) becomes

$$\boxed{x^2 \frac{d^2v}{dx^2} + AV = \frac{Q(x)X^2}{u(x)}} \qquad (3.26)$$

   a Cauchy equation.

3.10.1 CHANGE OF INDEPENDENT VARIABLE

Let $\quad \frac{dy}{dx} = \frac{dy}{dz}\frac{dz}{dx}$

and $\quad \frac{d^2y}{dx^2} = \frac{d^2y}{dz^2}\left(\frac{dz}{dx}\right)^2 + \frac{dy}{dz}\frac{d^2z}{dx^2}.$

Then (3.23) becomes

$$\frac{d^2y}{dz^2} + \frac{\dfrac{d^2z}{dx^2} + R(x)\dfrac{dz}{dx}}{\left(\dfrac{dz}{dx}\right)^2}\frac{dy}{dz} + \frac{S(x)y}{\left(\dfrac{dz}{dx}\right)^2} = \frac{Q(x)}{\left(\dfrac{dz}{dx}\right)^2} \qquad (3.27)$$

choose $\sqrt{\dfrac{\pm S(x)}{a^2}}$ so that it is a real number (a^2 can be chosen as 1).

The transformation

$$z = \int \sqrt{\frac{\pm S(x)}{a^2}}\ dx$$

reduces (3.27) to

$$\frac{d^2y}{dz^2} + A\frac{dy}{dz} \pm a^2 y = \frac{Q(x)}{\left(\dfrac{dz}{dx}\right)^2} \qquad (3.28)$$

a linear equation with constant coefficients.

CHAPTER 4

SERIES SOLUTIONS

4.1 POWER SERIES

1. A power series $\sum\limits_{n=0}^{\infty} a_n(x-x_0)^n$ is said to converge at a point x if

$$\lim_{m\to\infty} \sum_{n=0}^{m} a_n(x-x_0)^n \text{ exists.}$$

2. Ratio Test For Convergence

Compute

$$\lim_{n\to\infty} \left| \frac{a_{n+1}(x-x_0)^{n+1}}{a_n(x-x_0)^n} \right| = |x-x_0| \lim_{n\to\infty} \left| \frac{a_{n+1}}{a_n} \right| = L.$$

If:

L < 1, convergence exists

L > 1 or ∞, divergence exists

L = 1, no conclusion can be made

3. There is a number $\rho \geq 0$, called the radius of convergence, such that $\sum\limits_{n=0}^{\infty} a_n(x-x_0)^n$ converges absolutely for $|x-x_0| < \rho$ and diverges for $|x-x_0| > \rho$.

4. Addition and Subtraction

$$f(x) \pm g(x) = \sum_{n=0}^{\infty} (a_n \pm b_n)(x-x_0)^n$$

5. Multiplication

$$f(x)g(x) = [\sum_{n=0}^{\infty} a_n(x-x_0)^n][\sum_{n=0}^{\infty} b_n(x-x_0)^n]$$

$$= \sum_{n=0}^{\infty} c_n(x-x_0)^n$$

6. Division

$$\frac{f(x)}{g(x)} = \sum_{n=0}^{\infty} d_n(x-x_0)^n$$

For $g(x_0) \neq 0$

7. Differentiation

$$f'(x) = \sum_{n=1}^{\infty} na_n(x-x_0)^{n-1}$$

8. The value of a_n is given by

$$a_n = \frac{f^{(n)}(x_0)}{n!} \quad .$$

9. Shift of Index of Summation

Example:

$$\sum_{n=2}^{\infty} a_n x^n = \sum_{m=0}^{\infty} a_{m+2} x^{m+2} = \sum_{n=0}^{\infty} a_{n+2} x^{n+2}$$

10. Taylor Series Expansion About a Point x_0

$$\sum_{n=0}^{\infty} \frac{f^n(x_0)(x-x_0)^n}{n!} = f(x_0) + f'(x_0)(x-x_0) + \frac{f''(x_0)(x-x_0)^2}{2!} + \ldots$$

4.2 SERIES SOLUTIONS NEAR AN ORDINARY POINT

Consider the equation

$$P(x)y'' + Q(x)y' + R(x)y = 0. \tag{4.1}$$

1. A function is said to be analytic at a point x_0. If the Taylor series about x_0,

$$\sum_{n=0}^{\infty} \frac{f^{(n)}(x_0)}{n!} (x-x_0)^n,$$

   exists and converges to $f(x)$ for all x.

2. If the functions

$$p = \frac{Q(x)}{P(x)}$$

   and

$$q = \frac{R(x)}{P(x)}$$

   are analytic at x_0, then x_0 is an ordinary point, otherwise, it is a singular point.

3. If x_0 is an ordinary point of (4.1), then this equation has two linearly independent power series solutions of the form

$$\sum_{n=0}^{\infty} c_n(x-x_0)^n.$$

Procedure

1. Assume that the solution is of the form

$$y = \sum_{n=0}^{\infty} a_n(x-x_0)^n. \tag{4.2}$$

2. Substitute (4.2) and its derivatives into (4.1).

3. Collect all terms with the same powers of x.

4. Combine the equations to obtain the recurrence formula, a relation between the coefficients a_k and a_{k+1}.

5. Find the first few terms in the series.

6. Rewrite the general solution as

$$y = \sum_{n=0}^{\infty} a_n (x-x_0)^n = a_0 y_1(x) + a_1 y_2(x),$$

where a_0 and a_1 are arbitrary, and y_1 and y_2 are linearly independent series solutions.

4.3 REGULAR SINGULAR POINT

Consider the equation

$$P(x)y'' + Q(x)y' + R(x)y = 0. \tag{4.1}$$

x_0 is a regular singular point if:

1. It is a singular point.

2. Both

$$(x-x_0) \frac{Q(x)}{P(x)} \quad \text{and} \quad (x-x_0)^2 \frac{R(x)}{P(x)}$$

Have convergent Taylor series about x_0.

Otherwise, it is an irregular singular point.

4.4 SERIES SOLUTION NEAR A REGULAR SINGULAR POINT

Consider the equation

$$y'' + P(x)y' + Q(x)y = 0 \qquad (4.2)$$

(Let $x = 0$ be a regular singular point.)

Solution:

1. Assume the solution is of the form

$$y = x^r \sum_{n=0}^{\infty} a_n x^n = \sum_{n=0}^{\infty} a_n x^{r+n} \qquad (4.3)$$

2. Obtain y' and y'' of (4.3), then substitute into (4.2).

3. Simplify and collect the x^r terms, which gives the indicial equation

$$F(r) = r(r-1) + p_0 r + q_0 = 0 \qquad (4.4)$$

    where

$$p_0 = \lim_{x \to 0} x \frac{Q(x)}{P(x)}$$

$$q_0 = \lim_{x \to 0} x^2 \frac{R(x)}{P(x)} \qquad (4.5)$$

4. The roots of (4.4) are r_1 and r_2, with $r_1 > r_2$. These roots are called the exponents of the singularity.

5. Combining the coefficients of x^{r+n} terms gives the recurrence formula for a_n. For each root r_1 and r_2, use the recurrence formula to determine a_n separately.

6. If $r_1 = r_2 \neq$ integer or zero,

$$y_1(x) = |x|^{r_1}[1 + \sum_{n=1}^{\infty} a_n(r_1)x^n]$$

and

$$y_2(x) = |x|^{r_2}[1 + \sum_{n=1}^{\infty} a_n(r_2)x^n]$$

7. If $r_1 = r_2$,

$$y_1(x) = |x|^{r_1}[1 + \sum_{n=1}^{\infty} a_n(r_1)x^n]$$

and

$$y_2(x) = y_1(x)\ln|x| + |x|^{r_1}\sum_{n=1}^{\infty} a_n(r_1)x^n$$

8. If $r_1 - r_2$ = integer (positive),

$$y_1(x) = |x|^{r_1}[1 + \sum_{n=1}^{\infty} a_n(r_1)x^n]$$

and

$$y_2(x) = ay_1(x)\ln|x| + |x|^{r_2}[1 + \sum_{n=1}^{\infty} x^n \frac{d}{dr}[(r_1 - r_2)a_n(r)]\Big|_{r=r_2}]$$

4.5 EULER EQUATIONS

Consider an Euler equation of the general form

$$x^2 y'' + \alpha x y' + \beta y = 0 \tag{4.6}$$

and its indicial equation

$$F(r) = r(r-1) + \alpha r + \beta \tag{4.7}$$

The roots of (4.7) are

and

$$r_1 = \frac{-(\alpha-1)+((\alpha-1)^2-4\beta)^{\frac{1}{2}}}{2}$$

$$r_2 = \frac{-(\alpha-1)-((\alpha-1)^2-4\beta)^{\frac{1}{2}}}{2}$$

(4.8)

1. If $(\alpha-1)^2 - 4\beta > 0$,

$$y = c_1|x|^{r_1} + c_2|x|^{r_2}, \ (x>0)$$

If r_1 is not a rational number, then $x^{r_1} = e^{r_1 \ln x}$.

2. If $(\alpha-1)^2 - 4\beta = 0$,

$$r_1 = r_2 = \frac{-(\alpha-1)}{2}$$

and

$$y = (c_1 + c_2 \ln|x|)|x|^{r_1}, \ x > 0$$

3. If $(\alpha-1)^2 - 4\beta < 0$,

$$y = c_1|x|^{\lambda}\cos(\mu\ln|x|)+c_2|x|^{\lambda}\sin(\mu\ln|x|) \ (r_1 \& r_2 = \lambda \pm i\,\mu)$$

4.6 BESSEL'S EQUATION

Consider Bessel's equation of order P and of the general formula

$$x^2 \frac{d^2y}{dx^2} + x \frac{dy}{dx} + (x^2 - p^2)y = 0 \qquad (4.9)$$

Any solution of (4.9) is called Bessel's function of order p.

The Gamma Function of Bessel's Equation is

$$\Gamma(N) = \int_0^\infty e^{-x} x^{N-1} \, dx, \text{ for } N > 0.$$

The indicial equation of (4.9) is

$$r^2 - p^2 = 0.$$

The roots are $r_1 = p > 0$
and $r_2 = -p$
For $r_1 = p > 0$,

$$J_p(x) = \sum_{n=0}^\infty \frac{(-1)^n}{n!(n+p)!} \left(\frac{x}{2}\right)^{2n+p} \qquad (4.10)$$

where $(n+p)!$ is defined by $\Gamma(n+p+1)$. If p is not a positive integer.

For $r_2 = -p$,

$$J_{-p}(x) = \sum_{n=0}^\infty \frac{(-1)^n}{n!(n-p)!} \left(\frac{x}{2}\right)^{2n-p} \qquad (4.11)$$

where $(x-p)!$ is defined by $\Gamma(n-p+1)$.

If $p > 0$ is unequal to a positive integer, then

$$y = c_1 J_p(x) + c_2 J_{-p}(x) \qquad (4.12)$$

is the general solution to (4.9).

If p is a positive integer,

$$Y_p(x) = \frac{2}{\pi} \left\{ (\ln \frac{x}{2} + \gamma) J_p(x) - \frac{1}{2} \sum_{n=0}^{p-1} \frac{(p-n-1)!}{n!} \left(\frac{x}{2}\right)^{2n-p} \right. $$

$$\left. + \frac{1}{2} \sum_{n=0}^{\infty} (-1)^{n+1} \left(\sum_{k=1}^{n} \frac{1}{k} + \sum_{k=1}^{n+p} \frac{1}{k} \right) \left[\frac{1}{n!(n+p)!} \left(\frac{x}{2}\right)^{2n+p} \right] \right\}$$

and

$$y = c_1 J_p(x) + c_2 Y_p(x) \qquad (4.13)$$

is the general solution to (4.9).

γ is the Euler-Mascheroni constant

$$\gamma = \lim_{n \to \infty} (\mu_n - \ln n) \cong 0.5772.$$

Specific Cases

4.6.1 BESSEL'S EQUATION OF ORDER ZERO

$$x^2 y'' + xy' + x^2 y = 0, \quad r_1 = r_2 = 0 \qquad (4.14)$$

General Solution:

$$y = c_1 J_0(x) + c_2 Y_0(x)$$

where

$$J_0(x) = \left[1 + \sum_{m=1}^{\infty} \frac{(-1)^m x^{2m}}{2^{2m}(m!)^2} \right],$$

$$Y_0(x) = \frac{2}{\pi} \left[(\gamma + \ln \frac{x}{2}) J_0(x) + \sum_{m=1}^{\infty} \frac{(-1)^{m+1} \mu_m}{2^{2m}(m!)^2} x^{2m} \right]$$

(4.15)

and

$$\mu_m = \frac{1}{m} + \frac{1}{m-1} + \ldots + \frac{1}{2} + 1$$

4.6.2 BESSEL'S EQUATION OF ORDER 1/2

$$x^2y'' + xy' + (x^2 - \tfrac{1}{4})y = 0, \qquad (4.16)$$

$r_1\text{-}r_2$ = Positive Integer

∴ No log term in the 2nd solution

General Solution:

$$y = c_1 J_{\frac{1}{2}}(x) + c_2 J_{-\frac{1}{2}}(x)$$

$$J_{\frac{1}{2}}(x) = \left(\frac{2}{\pi x}\right)^{\frac{1}{2}} \sin x, \quad x > 0$$

$$J_{-\frac{1}{2}}(x) = \left(\frac{2}{\pi x}\right)^{\frac{1}{2}} \cos x, \quad x > 0$$

$$(4.17)$$

4.6.3 BESSEL'S EQUATION OF ORDER ONE

$$x^2y'' + xy' + (x^2-1)y = 0 \qquad (4.18)$$

General Solution:

$$y = c_1 J_1(x) + c_2 Y_1(x)$$

$$J_1(x) = \frac{x}{2} \sum_{m=0}^{\infty} \frac{(-1)^m x^{2m}}{2^{2m}(m+1)!\,m!}$$

$$Y_1(x) = \frac{2}{\pi} \left[-y_2(x) + (\gamma - \ln 2)J_1(x) \right]$$

$$(4.19)$$

$$y_2(x) = -J_1(x)\ln x + \frac{1}{x}\left[1 - \sum_{m=1}^{\infty} \frac{(-1)^m(\mu_m - \mu_{m-1})}{2^{2m}m!(m-1)!} x^{2m}\right]$$

$$x > 0$$

4.7 LEGENDRE'S DIFFERENTIAL EQUATIONS

Consider the equation

$$(1-x^2)y'' - 2xy' + \lambda(\lambda+1)y = 0, \text{ where} \qquad (4.20)$$

λ is a constant. This is called Legendre's Differential Equation.

$x = 0$ is an ordinary point for the equation.

$x = \pm 1$ are regular singular points for the equation.

The series solution around the point $x = 0$ is

$$y(x) = \sum_{n=0}^{\infty} c_n x^n.$$

The recurrence formula is

$$c_n = \frac{(n-1)(n-2) - \lambda(\lambda+1)}{n(n-1)} c_{n-2}, \quad n \geq 2.$$

The general solution is

$$y(x) = c_0 y_0(x) + c_1 y_1(x),$$

$$y_0 = 1 - \frac{\lambda(\lambda+1)}{2!} x^2 + \frac{\lambda(\lambda+1)(\lambda-2)(\lambda+3)}{4!} x^4$$

$$- \frac{\lambda(\lambda+1)(\lambda-2)(\lambda+3)(\lambda-4)(\lambda+5)}{6!} x^6 + \ldots,$$

and

$$y_1 = x - \frac{(\lambda-1)(\lambda+2)}{3!} x^3 + \frac{(\lambda-1)(\lambda+2)(\lambda-3)(\lambda+4)}{5!} x^5 + \ldots$$

$$(4.21)$$

4.8 GUASS' HYPERGEOMETRIC EQUATION

Consider Gauss' Hypergeometric Equation

$$x(1-x)y'' + [c-(a+b+1)x]y' - aby = 0. \tag{4.22}$$

$x = 0$, $x = 1$ are regular singular points.

Assume a series solution of the form

$$y = \sum_{n=0}^{\infty} d_n x^{n+r}. \tag{4.23}$$

The indicial equation for (4.22) is

$$r(r-(1-c))d_n x^r = 0. \tag{4.24}$$

The recurrence formula for (4.22) is

$$d_{n+1} = \frac{(b+n)(n+a)}{(n+1)(n+c)} c_n \tag{4.25}$$

The roots of (4.24) are

and

$$r_1 = 0$$

$$r_2 = (1-c).\tag{4.26}$$

Substituting (4.26) into (4.23) yields the general solution

$$y_1 = 1 + \sum_{n=0}^{\infty} \frac{a(a+1)\ldots(a+n-1)b(b+1)\ldots(b+n-1)x^n}{n!\,c(c+1)\ldots(c+n-1)}$$

$$\tag{4.27}$$

For $r_1 = 0$.

y_1 is known as the hypergeometric series.

For $r_2 = (1-c)$, the particular solution is

$$y_2 = B_0 x^{1-c} \left\{ 1 + \sum_{n=1}^{\infty} \frac{[(a-c+1)(a-c+2)\ldots(a-c+n)]}{(1\cdot 2\ldots n)} \right. $$
$$\left. + \frac{[(b-c+1)(b-c+2)\ldots(b-c+n)]}{[(2-c)(3-c)\ldots(n+1-c)]} \right\} \tag{4.28}$$

The general solution to (4.22) is

$$y = c_1 y_1 + c_2 y_2$$

CHAPTER 5

HIGHER ORDER LINEAR EQUATIONS

5.1 GENERAL THEORY

Consider the general equation

$$a_0(x) \frac{d^n y}{dx^n} + a_1(x) \frac{d^{n-1} y}{dx^{n-1}} + \ldots + a_{n-1}(x) \frac{dy}{dx} + a_n(x)y = F(x). \quad (5.1)$$

Let $a_0 \ldots a_n$ and F be continuous real-valued functions on some interval $\alpha < x < \beta$.

Also, let a_0 be not identically zero.

Then, if $F(x) = 0$, (5.1) is called homogeneous.

Further, let $f_1, f_2, \ldots, f_m$ be m solutions of

$$a_0(x)y^n + a_1(x)y^{n-1} + \ldots + a_{n-1}(x)y' + a_n(x)y = 0. \quad (5.2)$$

Then

$$c_1 f_1 + c_2 f_2 + c_3 f_3 + \ldots + c_m f_m$$

is also a solution of (5.2).

The m functions $f_1, f_2, \ldots, f_m$ are called linearly dependent if there exists constants $c_1, c_2, \ldots, c_m$, not all zero, such that

38

$$c_1 f_1(x) + c_2 f_2(x) + \ldots + c_m f_m(x) = 0.$$

Alternatively, $f_1, f_2, \ldots, f_m$ are linearly independent if

$$w(f_1, f_2, \ldots f_m) = \begin{vmatrix} f_1 & f_2 & \ldots & f_m \\ f'_1 & f'_2 & \ldots & f'_m \\ f_1^{(m-1)} & f_2^{(m-1)} & \ldots f_m^{(m-1)} \end{vmatrix} \neq 0.$$

5.2 HOMOGENEOUS EQUATIONS WITH CONSTANT COEFFICIENTS

Consider the general equation

$$a_0 \frac{d^n y}{dx^n} + a_1 \frac{d^{n-1} y}{dx^{n-1}} + \ldots + a_{n-1} \frac{dy}{dx} + a_n y = 0 \tag{5.2}$$

and its characteristic equation

$$a_0 m^n + a_1 m^{n-1} + \ldots + a_{n-1} m + a_n = 0. \tag{5.3}$$

If the characteristic equation has:

1. Real and unequal roots, then

$$\boxed{y = c_1 e^{m_1 x} + c_2 e^{m_2 x} + \ldots + c_n e^{m_n x}} \tag{5.4}$$

is the solution for the general equation.

2. Repeated roots (real roots m occurring k times), then the general solution is

$$\boxed{y = (c_1 + c_2 x + c_3 x^2 + \ldots + c_k x^{k-1}) e^{mx}} \tag{5.5}$$

2a. Repeated roots (see above) plus remaining roots that are distinct real roots $(m_{k+1}, \ldots m_n)$, then the general solution is

$$y = (c_1 + c_2 x + c_3 x^2 + \ldots + c_k x^{k-1})\, e^{mx} + c_{k+1}\, e^{m_{k+1} x} + \ldots + c_n e^{m_n x}$$

(5.6)

3. Complex roots $(m_1 = a + bi,\ m_2 = a - bi)$, then the general solution is

$$y = e^{ax}(c_1 \sin bx + c_2 \cos bx)$$

(5.7)

5.3 METHOD OF UNDETERMINED COEFFICIENTS

Consider the general equation

$$a_0 \frac{d^n y}{dx^n} + a_1 \frac{d^{n-1} y}{dx^{n-1}} + \ldots + a_{n-1}\frac{dy}{dx} + a_n y = f(x).$$

(5.1)

The general solution is

$$y = y_c + y_p$$

where

y_c = complementary solution of homogeneous equation,

y_p = particular solution.

To find y_p, substitute $y_p(x)$ and its derivatives into (5.1) according to the form of $f(x)$. Solve for the coefficients by equating equal powers of x.

$f(x)$	$y_p(x)$
$P_m(x) = b_0 x^m + b_1 x^{m-1} + \ldots + b_m$	$x^s(A_0 x^m + \ldots + A_m)$
$P_m(x)e^{\alpha x}$	$x^s(A_0 x^m + \ldots + A_m)e^{\alpha x}$
$P_m(x)e^{\alpha x}\begin{cases} \sin\beta x \\ \cos\beta x \end{cases}$	$x^s[(A_0 x^m + \ldots + A_m)e^{\alpha x}\cos\beta x$ $+(B_0 x^m + \ldots + B_m)e^{\alpha x}\sin\beta x]$

s is the smallest non-negative integer for which every term in $y_p(x)$ differs from every term in the function $y_c(x)$

5.4 VARIATION OF PARAMETERS

Consider the general equation

$$a_0 \frac{d^n y}{dx^n} + a_1 \frac{d^{n-1}y}{dx^{n-1}} + \ldots + a_{n-1}\frac{dy}{dx} + a_n y = f(x) \qquad (5.1)$$

Suppose that a fundamental set of solutions $y_1, y_2, \ldots, y_n$ is known. A particular solution takes the form

$$y_p(x) = u_1(x)y_1(x) + u_2(x)y_2(x) + \ldots + u_n(x)y_n(x) \qquad (5.8)$$

where

$$u'_m(x) = \frac{f(x)W_m(x)}{W(x)} \quad , \quad m = 1, 2, \ldots, n,$$

$$W(x) = W(y_1, y_2, \ldots, y_n)(x).$$

$W_m(x)$ is the determinant obtained from $W(y_1, y_2, \ldots, y_n)$ by replacing the mth column by the column $(0, 0, \ldots, 0, 1)$

$$(5.9)$$

$$\therefore \boxed{y_p(x) = \sum_{m=1}^{n} y_m(x) \int \frac{f(x)W_m(x)}{W(x)} \, dx} \qquad (5.10)$$

is the general solution to (5.1).

5.5 LINEAR EQUATIONS WITH CONSTANT COEFFICIENTS

In operator form, consider the equation

$$F(D)y = (P_0 D^n + P_1 D^{n-1} + \dots + P_{n-1}D + P_n)y = Q(x). \qquad (5.11)$$

Let

$$\frac{1}{F(D)}$$

be defined

$$\frac{1}{F(D)} \cdot F(D)y = y.$$

Then

$$y = \frac{1}{D-m_1} \cdot \frac{1}{D-m_2} \cdot \frac{1}{D-m_3} \cdots \frac{1}{D-m_n} Q. \qquad (5.12)$$

5.5.1 FIRST METHOD OF SOLUTION

$$\boxed{y = e^{m_1 x} \int e^{(m_2 - m_1)x} \int e^{(m_3 - m_2)x} \int \\ \cdots \int e^{(m_n - m_{n-1})x} \int Q e^{-m_n x} \, (dx)^n}$$

$$(5.13)$$

5.5.2 SECOND METHOD OF SOLUTION

$$y = N_1 e^{m_1 x} \int Q e^{-m_1 x} dx + N_2 e^{m_2 x} \int Q e^{-m_2 x} dx$$

$$+ \ldots + N_n e^{m_n x} \int Q e^{-m_n x} dx$$

(5.14)

where $\dfrac{1}{F(D)}$ is expressed as the sum of n partial fractions:

$$\frac{N_1}{D-m_1} + \frac{N_2}{D-m_2} + \ldots + \frac{N_n}{D-m_n}.$$

5.6 SHORT METHOD

A linear differential equation

$$F(D)y = Q$$

(5.15)

has a particular integral

$$y = \frac{1}{F(D)} Q.$$

a) If Q is of the form e^{ax},

$$y = \frac{1}{F(a)} e^{ax}, \quad F(a) \neq 0$$

(5.16)

b) If Q is of the form x^m,

$$y = (a_0 + a_1 D + a_2 D^2 + \ldots + a_m D^m) x^m, \quad a_0 \neq 0$$

(5.17)

43

c) If Q is of the form sin(ax+b) or cos(ax+b),

$$y = \frac{1}{F(-a^2)} \sin(ax+b), \quad F(-a^2) \neq 0$$
or
$$y = \frac{1}{F(-a^2)} \cos(ax+b), \quad F(-a^2) \neq 0$$

(5.18)

d) If Q is of the form $e^{ax}V(x)$,

$$y = \frac{1}{F(D)} e^{ax}V = e^{ax} \frac{1}{F(D+a)} V$$

(5.19)

e) If Q is of the form $xV(x)$,

$$y = x \frac{1}{F(D)} V - \frac{F'(D)}{\{F(D)\}^2} V$$

(5.20)

5.7 CAUCHY LINEAR EQUATION

Consider a Cauchy Linear Equation of the general form

(5.21)

$$a_0 x^n \frac{d^n y}{dx^n} + a_1 x^{n-1}\frac{d^{n-1}y}{dx^{n-1}} +\ldots+ a_{n-1} \frac{xdy}{dx}+a_n y = F(x)$$

The transformation $x = e^t$ reduces (5.21) such that

$$\frac{dy}{dx} = \frac{1}{x} \frac{dy}{dt}$$

$$\frac{d^2y}{dx^2} = \frac{1}{x^2}\left(\frac{d^2y}{dt^2} - \frac{dy}{dt}\right)$$

44

$$\frac{d^3y}{dx^2} = \frac{1}{x^3}\left[\frac{d^3y}{dx^3} - 3\frac{d^2y}{dt^2} + 2\frac{dy}{dt}\right]$$

$$\vdots$$

To find the expression for $x^n \dfrac{d^n y}{dx^n}$:

1) Determine

$$r(r-1)(r-2)\ldots[r-(n-1)], \ r > 0.$$

2) Expand the above as a polynomial of degree n in r.

3) Replace r^k by $\dfrac{d^k y}{dx^k}$, for each $k = 1,2,3,\ldots,n$.

4) Equate

$$x^n \frac{d^n y}{dx^n}$$

to the result in Step 3.

Substitute into (5.21) to make it a linear equation with constant coefficients.

5.8 LEGENDRE LINEAR EQUATION

Consider the Legendre Linear Equation of the general form

$$P_0(ax+b)^n \frac{d^n x}{dx^n} + P_1(ax+b)^{n-1}\frac{d^{n-1}y}{dx^{n-1}} +\ldots+ P_{n-1}(ax+b)\frac{dy}{dx}$$

$$+ P_n y = Q(x).$$

Let $ax + b = e^z$. Then

$$(ax+b)^r D^r y = a^r \theta(\theta-1)\ldots(\theta-r+1)y.$$

The Legendre equation becomes

$$\{P_0a^n \theta(\theta-1)(\theta-2)\ldots(\theta-n+1)+p_1a^{n-1}\theta(\theta-1)(\theta-z)\ldots$$

$$(\theta-n+2)+\ldots+P_{n-1}\,a\theta+p_n\}y=Q\left(\frac{e^z-b}{a}\right),$$

A linear equation with constant coefficients.

5.9 TOTAL DIFFERENTIAL EQUATIONS

Consider the equation

$$P(x,y,z,\ldots,t)dx+Q(x,y,z,\ldots t)dy+\ldots+s(x,y,z,\ldots t)dt=0.$$

5.9.1 CONDITION OF INTEGRABILITY

Consider

$$P(x,y,z)dx + Q(x,y,z)dy + R(x,y,z)dz = 0 \qquad (5.22)$$

The condition is

$$P\left(\frac{\partial Q}{\partial z} - \frac{\partial R}{\partial y}\right) + Q\left(\frac{\partial R}{\partial x} - \frac{\partial P}{\partial z}\right) + R\left(\frac{\partial P}{\partial y} - \frac{\partial Q}{\partial x}\right) = 0. \qquad (5.23)$$

5.9.2 CONDITION FOR EXACTNESS

$$\frac{\partial P}{\partial y} = \frac{\partial Q}{\partial x}, \quad \frac{\partial Q}{\partial z} = \frac{\partial R}{\partial y}, \quad \frac{\partial R}{\partial x} = \frac{\partial P}{\partial z}$$

Procedure

1. If the equation is exact, follow the previous procedure.

2. If the equation is not exact, use an integrating factor.

3. If the equation is homogeneous, a variable, say z, can be separated: $x = uz$, $y = vz$.

4. If no integrating factor can be found, consider one of the variables, say z, as a constant. Integrate the equation. Denote the arbitrary constant as $\phi(z)$. Take the total differential of the integral and solve for $\phi(z)$. Solve for the other variables in the same manner.

5.10 ADJOINT EQUATIONS

The adjoint equation to

$$(5.24)$$

$$a_0(x) \frac{d^n y}{dx^n} + a_1(x) \frac{d^{n-1} y}{dx^{n-1}} + \ldots + a_{n-1}(x) \frac{dy}{dx} + a_n(x)y = 0$$

is the equation

$$(-1)^n \frac{d^n}{dx^n}[a_0(x)y] + (-1)^{n-1} \frac{d^{n-1}}{dx^{n-1}}[a_1(x)y] + \ldots$$

$$- \frac{d}{dx}[a_{n-1}(x)y] + a_n(x)y = 0$$

$$(5.25)$$

5.10.1 SECOND-ORDER CASE

The adjoint equation to

$$a_0(x) \frac{d^2 y}{dx^2} + a_1(x) \frac{dy}{dx} + a_2(x)y = 0 \qquad (5.26)$$

is

$$(5.27)$$

$$a_0(x) \frac{d^2 y}{dx^2} + [2a'(x) - a_1(x)] \frac{dy}{dx} + [a_0''(x) - a_1'(x) + a_2(x)]y = 0$$

Consider the Differential Operator

$$L_n = a_0(x) \frac{d^n}{dx^n} + a_1(x) \frac{d^{n-1}}{dx^{n-1}} + \ldots + a_{n-1}(x) \frac{d}{dx} + a_n(x)$$

where the coefficients a_k have continuous $(n-k)+h$ derivatives $(k = 0, 1, 2, \ldots, n)$ on the interval $a \leq x \leq b$.

Let u and v be any two functions having nth derivatives on $a \leq x \leq L$.

$$vL_n[u] - u\bar{L}_n[v] = \frac{d}{dx}[P(u,v)] \qquad (5.28)$$

where

$\bar{L}_n$ is the adjoint operator,

$$P(u,v) = \sum_{k=1}^{n} \left[\sum_{j=1}^{k} (-1)^{j-1} u^{(k-j)} (v\, a_{n-k})^{(j-1)} \right]$$

and (for any two points x_1 and x_2 of $a \leq x \leq b$).

$$\int_{x_1}^{x_2} \{vL_n[u] - u\,\bar{L}_n[v]\}\, dx = P(u,v)\Big|_{x=x_2} - P(u,v)\Big|_{x=x_1}$$

This last equation is called Green's formula.

Equation (5.28) is called the Lagrange Identity.

5.10.2 SECOND-ORDER CASE

Consider the operator

$$L_2 = a_0(x)\, \frac{d^2}{dx^2} + a_1(x)\, \frac{d}{dx} + a_2(x).$$

According to (5.28),

$$v\, L_n[u] - u\, \bar{L}_n[v] = \frac{d}{dx}\, [a_0 vu' + (a_1 - a_0')vu - a_0 v'u].$$

f is a solution of the equation

$$L_n y = 0.$$

48

If it is a solution of the (n-1)st-order equation

$$P[y, g(x)] = c,$$

where   g = nontrivial solution of the adjoint equation.

$$\bar{L}_n y = 0,$$

and   c = arbitrary constant.

5.10.3 SECOND–ORDER CASE

Consider equation (5.26). f is a solution to (5.26) if and only if it is a solution to

$$a_0(x)g(x)\frac{dy}{dx} + \{[a_1(x) - a_0'(x)]g(x) - a_0(x)g'(x)\}y = c.$$

5.10.4 SELF–ADJOINT EQUATIONS

If an equation is identical to its adjoint equation, then it is called self-adjoint.

5.10.5 SECOND–ORDER CASE

Equation (5.26) is self-adjoint if

$$\frac{d}{dx}[a_0(x)] = a_1(x).$$

Also, equation (5.26) can be transformed into the equivalent self-adjoint equation

$$\boxed{\frac{d}{dx}[P(x)\frac{dy}{dx}] + Q(x)y = 0}$$

where

$$P(x) = \exp\left[\int \frac{a_1(x)}{a_0(x)}\,dx\right],$$

49

$$Q(x) = \frac{a_2(x)}{a_0(x)} \exp\left[\int \frac{a_1(x)}{a_0(x)} dx\right]$$

By multiplying by the factor

$$\frac{1}{a_0(x)} \exp\left[\int \frac{a_1(x)}{a_0(x)} dx\right]$$

5.11 THE STURM THEOREM

5.11.1 ABEL'S FORMULA

Let f and g be any two solutions of

$$\frac{d}{dx}[P(x)\frac{dy}{dx}] + Q(x)y = 0 \qquad (5.30)$$

where P has continuous derivative, Q is continuous, and $P(x) > 0$ on $a \leq x \leq L$.

Then

$$P(x)[f(x)g'(x) - f'(x)g(x)] = k \qquad (5.31)$$

for all x on $a \leq x \leq b$

where k is a constant.

5.11.2 STURM SEPARATION THEOREM

Consider equation (5.30) with f and g as independent solutions.

Between any two consecutive zeros of f there is precisely one zero of g.

5.11.3 STURM'S FUNDAMENTAL COMPARISON THEOREM

Let ϕ_1 be a real solution of

$$\frac{d}{dx}\left[P(x)\frac{dy}{dx}\right] + Q_1(x)y = 0 \qquad\qquad (5.32)$$

and ϕ_2 be a real solution of

$$\frac{d}{dx}\left[P(x)\frac{dy}{dx}\right] + Q_2(x)y = 0. \qquad\qquad (5.33)$$

Also let $P(x) > 0$ and $Q_2(x) > Q_1(x)$.

Then, if x_1 and x_2 are successive zeros of ϕ_1, ϕ_2 has at least one zero at some point of the interval $x_1 < x < x_2$.

CHAPTER 6

SYSTEMS OF LINEAR EQUATIONS

6.1 SOLUTIONS OF LINEAR SYSTEMS BY ELIMINATION

The elimination method for solving linear systems can be used:

1. Efficiently for systems of only two or three first-order equations.

2. For homogeneous and non-homogeneous equations.

3. As an advantage in some problems involving systems of higher-order equations.

Consider the system

$$L_1 x + L_2 y = f_1(t), \tag{6.1}$$

$$L_3 x + L_4 y = f_2(t) \tag{6.2}$$

Apply L_4 to (6.1) and L_2 to (6.2):

$$L_4 L_1 x + L_4 L_2 y = L_4 f_1, \tag{6.3}$$

$$L_2 L_3 x + L_2 L_4 y = L_2 f_2. \tag{6.4}$$

Subtract (6.4) from (6.3):

$$(L_1 L_4 - L_2 L_3)x = L_4 f_1 - L_2 f_2 \qquad (6.5)$$

In another form,

$$L_5 x = g,$$

Solve for x:

$$x = c_1 u_1 + c_2 u_2 + \ldots + c_n u_n + U, \qquad (6.6)$$

Repeat the procedure (apply L_3 to (6.1) and L_1 to (6.2)) and solve for y:

$$y = k_1 u_1 + k_2 u_2 + \ldots + k_n u_n + U_2. \qquad (6.7)$$

The number of independent constants in the general solutions (6.6) and (6.7) is equal to the order of

$$\begin{vmatrix} L_1 & L_2 \\ L_3 & L_4 \end{vmatrix}$$

6.2 SYSTEMS OF LINEAR ALGEBRAIC EQUATIONS

Given that $Ax = b$:

If $b = 0$, the system is homogeneous. Otherwise, it is non-homogeneous.

If Det A is not zero, then A is nonsingular and A^{-1} exists:

$$x = A^{-1}b.$$

Solution Procedure

1. Write systems of equations in matrix and vector form.

2. Transform the coefficient matrix into triangular form.

3. Write the corresponding system of equations.

4. Solve for the components of x.

If A is singular then the solutions of Ax = b either do not exist, or do exist but are not unique.

Another condition is that $(b,y) = 0$, such that y satisfies $A*y = 0$ where A* is the adjoint of A.

Each solution has the form

$$x = x^{(0)} + \xi ,$$

where $x^{(0)}$ is a particular solution of

$$Ax = b$$

and ξ is any solution of

$$Ax = 0.$$

6.3 MATRICES AND VECTORS

A is an m × n matrix

$$A = \begin{pmatrix} a_{11} & a_{12} \cdots & a_{1n} \\ a_{21} & a_{22} \cdots & a_{2n} \\ \vdots & \vdots & \vdots \\ a_{m_1} & a_{m_2} \cdots & a_{mn} \end{pmatrix}$$

An element in the ith row and jth column is called a_{ij}.

An n × n matrix is a square matrix.

An n × 1 matrix is a vector.

A^T is the Transpose of A.

$\overline{A}$ is the Conjugate of A.

adj A is the Adjoint of A

Example for $A = \begin{pmatrix} 3 & 2-i \\ 4+3i & -5+2i \end{pmatrix}$,

$$A^T = \begin{pmatrix} 3 & 4+3i \\ 2-i & -5+2i \end{pmatrix}, \quad \text{adj } A = \begin{pmatrix} -5+2i & -2+i \\ -4-3i & 3 \end{pmatrix}$$

and $\overline{A} = \begin{pmatrix} 3 & 2+i \\ 4-3i & -5-2i \end{pmatrix}$.

$0 = \begin{pmatrix} 0 \\ 0 \\ 0 \end{pmatrix}$ is a zero vector.

Consider an n × n matrix A.

The Principal Diagonal is composed of elements from the upper left corner to the lower right corner of A.

An identity matrix is

$$I = \begin{pmatrix} 1 & 0 & 0 & 0 \\ 0 & 1 & 0 & 0 \\ 0 & 0 & 1 & 0 \\ 0 & 0 & 0 & 1 \end{pmatrix}$$

A square matrix A of real numbers is called a real symmetric matrix if $A^T = A$.

Properties

1. Equality: $a_{ij} = b_{ji}$

2. Addition: $A+B = (a_{ij})+(b_{ij}) = (a_{ij}+b_{ij})$; $A+B = B+A$

3. Multiplication:

$B = cA$ if $b_{ij} = ca_{ij}$

$\alpha(A+B) = \alpha A + \alpha B$

$(\alpha+\beta)A = \alpha A + \beta A$

$AB = C = [c_{ij}]$,

where

$$c_{ij} = \sum_{k=1}^{n} a_{ik}b_{kj} \quad (i=1,2,\ldots,n; \ j=1,2,\ldots,p)$$

For multiplicative the number of columns of A must equal the number of rows of B.

4. Subtraction: $A - B = A + (-B)$

5. Inverse: $AA^{-1} = A^{-1}A = I$

If A has a multiplicative inverse A^{-1}, then A is said to be nonsingular.

A has a singular cofactor c_{ij}, $c_{ij} = (-1)^{i+j}M_{ij}$

6.3.1 MATRIX FUNCTIONS

1. $\dfrac{dA}{dt} = \left(\dfrac{d(a_{ij})}{dt} \right)$

2. $\displaystyle\int_{a}^{b} A(t)\,dt = \left(\int_{a}^{b} a_{ij}(t)\,dt \right)$

3. $\dfrac{d}{dt}(cA) = c\dfrac{dA}{dt}$, where c is a constant matrix

4. $\dfrac{d}{dt}(A+B) = \dfrac{dA}{dt} + \dfrac{dB}{dt}$

5. $\dfrac{d}{dt}(AB) = \dfrac{dB}{dt}A + B\dfrac{dA}{dt}$.

Consider the equation

$$x' = P(t)x \qquad (6.8)$$

with

$$\Psi(t) = \begin{pmatrix} x_1^{(1)}(t) & \cdots & x_1^{(n)}(t) \\ \vdots & & \vdots \\ x_n^{(1)}(t) & \cdots & x_n^{(n)}(t) \end{pmatrix}$$

as a fundamental matrix.

The general solution of (6.8) is then

$$x = \psi(t)c.$$

with initial condition $x(t_0) = x^0$,

$$\boxed{x = \psi(t)\,\psi^{-1}(t_0)x^0}$$

or

$$\boxed{x = \phi(t)x^0}$$

To transform A into a diagonal matrix, use the transformation matrix

$$T = \begin{pmatrix} \xi_1^{(1)} & \cdots & \xi_{(1)}^{(n)} \\ \vdots & & \vdots \\ \xi_n^{(1)} & \cdots & \xi_n^{(n)} \end{pmatrix}$$

6.4 LINEAR INDEPENDENCE

Consider a set of n vectors

$$\begin{pmatrix} x_{11}c_1 + \ldots + x_{1n}c_n \\ \vdots \qquad\qquad \vdots \\ x_{n1}c_1 + \ldots + x_{nn}c_n \end{pmatrix} = x_c = 0. \qquad (6.9)$$

If Det $x \neq 0$, then (6.9) is linearly independent. If Det $x = 0$, then (6.9) is linearly dependent.

1. A system of n homogeneous linear algebraic equations in n unknowns has a non-trivial solution if and only if the determinant of the coefficients of the system is equal to zero.

2. A system of n linear algebraic equations in n unknowns has a unique solution if and only if the determinant of coefficients of the system is unequal to zero.

6.5 EIGENVALUES AND EIGENFUNCTIONS

Consider the equation

$$Ax = y. \qquad (6.10)$$

To solve (6.10), set

$$y = \lambda x$$

or

$$(A - \lambda I)x = 0$$

or

$$Det(A - \lambda I) = 0.$$

The values of λ obtained are called eigenvalues.

The solutions are called eigenfunctions.

$$\text{Let } A = \begin{pmatrix} a_{11} & a_{12} \ldots a_{1n} \\ a_{21} & a_{22} \ldots a_{2n} \\ \vdots & \vdots \qquad \vdots \\ a_{n1} & a_{n2} \ldots a_{nn} \end{pmatrix} \quad ; \quad x = \begin{pmatrix} x_1 \\ x_2 \\ \vdots \\ x_n \end{pmatrix}$$

To find λ,

Let

$$\text{Det} \begin{pmatrix} (a_{11} - \lambda) & a_{12} & \cdots & a_{1n} \\ a_{21} & (a_{22} - \lambda) & \cdots & \cdot \\ \vdots & & \vdots & \vdots \\ a_{n1} & \cdots & \cdots & (a_{nn} - \lambda) \end{pmatrix} = 0.$$

Expand and solve for λ.

Substitute λ into (6.10) to solve for x.

$$A* = A, \quad \text{or} \quad \overline{a}_{ji} = a_{ij},$$

is a self-adjoint or Hermitian matrix.

Let $AT = \begin{pmatrix} \lambda_1 x_1^{(1)} & \cdots & \lambda_n x_1^{(n)} \\ \vdots & & \vdots \\ \lambda_1 x_n^{(1)} & \cdots & \lambda_n x_n^{(n)} \end{pmatrix} = TD.$

If the eigenvalues and eigenfunctions of A are known, A can be transformed into a diagonal matrix by the process

$$T^{-1}AT = D.$$

The process is known as a similarity transformation.

Eigenvectors are determined up to an arbitrary multiplicative constant; if this constant is specified, then the eigenfunctions are said to be normalized.

6.6 BASIC THEORY OF SYSTEMS OF 1st ORDER LINEAR SYSTEMS

Consider the System

$$\frac{dx_1}{dt} = a_{11}(t)x_1 + a_{12}(t)x_2 + \ldots + a_{1n}(t)x_n + F_1(t),$$

$$\frac{dx_2}{dt} = a_{21}(t)x_1 + a_{22}(t)x_2 + \ldots + a_{2n}(t)x_n + F_2(t),$$

$$\vdots \qquad\qquad (6.11)$$

$$\frac{dx_n}{dt} = a_{n1}(t)x_1 + a_{n2}(t)x_2 + \ldots + a_{nn}(t)x_n + F_n(t).$$

Let

$$A(t) = \begin{pmatrix} a_{11}(t) & a_{12}(t) \ldots a_{1n}(t) \\ \vdots & \vdots \qquad\quad \vdots \\ a_{n1}(t) & a_{n2}(t) \ldots a_{nn}(t) \end{pmatrix},$$

$$F(t) = \begin{pmatrix} F_1(t) \\ F_2(t) \\ \vdots \\ F_n(t) \end{pmatrix}$$

and

$$x = \begin{pmatrix} x_1 \\ x_2 \\ \vdots \\ x_n \end{pmatrix}$$

Then (6.11) becomes

$$\frac{dx}{dt} = A(t)x + F(t). \qquad (6.12)$$

(6.12) is called a vector differential equation. The general solution of (6.12) is

$$x = \phi(t),$$

$$\phi(t) = \begin{pmatrix} \phi_1 \\ \phi_2 \\ \vdots \\ \phi_n \end{pmatrix}.$$

(6.12) has the same basic properties as the ordinary differential equation.

6.7 HOMOGENEOUS LINEAR SYSTEMS WITH CONSTANT COEFFICIENTS

6.7.1 TWO EQUATIONS IN TWO UNKNOWN FUNCTIONS

Consider

$$\frac{dx}{dt} = a_1 x + b_1 y$$

and   (6.13)

$$\frac{dy}{dt} = a_2 x + b_2 y.$$

The general form of the solution is

$$x = Ae^{\lambda t}$$

and

$$y = Be^{\lambda t}$$

The characteristic equation is

$$\lambda^2 - (a_1 + b_2)\lambda + (a_1 b_2 - a_2 b_1) = 0 \qquad (6.14)$$

The real and Distinct Roots are

$$x = c_1 A_1 e^{\lambda_1 t} + c_2 A_2 e^{\lambda_2 t}$$

and   (6.15)

$$y = c_1 B_1 e^{\lambda_1 t} + c_2 B_2 e^{\lambda_2 t}$$

The complex roots ($a \pm bi$) are

61

$$\boxed{\begin{aligned}
&x = e^{at}[c_1(A_1\cos bt - A_2\sin bt) + c_2(A_2\cos bt + A_1\sin bt)]\\
\text{and}\quad &y = e^{at}[c_1(B_1\cos bt - B_2\sin bt) + c_2(B_2\cos bt + B_1\sin bt)]
\end{aligned}}$$

(6.16)

The repeated roots are

$$\boxed{\begin{aligned}
&x = c_1 A e^{\lambda t} + c_2(A_1 t + A_2)e^{\lambda t}\\
\text{and}\quad &y = c_1 B e^{\lambda t} + c_2(B_1 t + B_2)e^{\lambda t}
\end{aligned}}$$

(6.17)

6.7.2 n EQUATIONS IN n UNKNOWN FUNCTIONS

Consider

$$\frac{dx_1}{dt} = a_{11}x_1 + a_{12}x_2 + \ldots + a_{1n}x_n,$$
$$\vdots$$
$$\frac{dx_2}{dt} = a_{21}x_1 + a_{22}x_2 + \ldots + a_{2n}x_n,$$

(6.13)

$$\vdots$$
$$\frac{dx_n}{dt} = a_{n1}x_1 + a_{n2}x_2 + \ldots + a_{nn}x_n,$$

which is written

$$\frac{dx}{dt} = Ax,$$

(6.14)

where

$$A = \begin{pmatrix}
a_{11} & a_{12} & \cdots & a_{1n}\\
a_{21} & a_{22} & \cdots & a_{2n}\\
\vdots & \vdots & & \vdots\\
a_{n1} & a_{n2} & \cdots & a_{nn}
\end{pmatrix}$$

and
$$x = \begin{pmatrix} x_1 \\ x_2 \\ \vdots \\ \dot{x}_n \end{pmatrix}.$$

A is called the coefficient matrix of (6.13).

General form of the solution is

$$\boxed{x = \alpha e^{\lambda t}} \qquad (6.15)$$

where
$$\alpha = \begin{pmatrix} \alpha_1 \\ \alpha_2 \\ \vdots \\ \alpha_n \end{pmatrix}.$$

(6.15) is reduced to

$$(A - \lambda I)\alpha = 0. \qquad (6.16)$$

Compute
$$|A - \lambda I| = 0,$$

or

$$\begin{vmatrix} a_{11} - \lambda & a_{12} & \cdots & a_{1n} \\ a_{21} & a_{22} - \lambda & \cdots & a_{2n} \\ \vdots & \vdots & & \vdots \\ a_{n_1} & a_{n_2} & \cdots & a_{nn} - \lambda \end{vmatrix} = 0, \text{ The charac-}$$
teristic equation.

The roots of this equation are the Eigenvalues $\lambda_1, \lambda_2, \ldots, \lambda_n$.

$$\alpha^{(i)} = \begin{pmatrix} \alpha_{1i} \\ \alpha_{2i} \\ \vdots \\ \alpha_{ni} \end{pmatrix} \qquad i = (1, 2, \ldots, n)$$

is the Eigenfunction corresponding to the Eigenvalues λ_i (i=1,2,...,n).

1. If all Eigenvalues are real and distinct,
$$x = \alpha^{(n)} e^{\lambda_n t}.$$

2. If there are complex roots,
$$x = \alpha^{(n)} e^{\lambda_n t}$$
with complex value solutions.

3. If the roots are repeated, the number of solutions is smaller than n. Additional solutions of another form are needed.

6.8 COMPLEX EIGENVALUES

Suppose $x' = Ax$. $\qquad\qquad$ (6.14)

If $\quad \lambda_1 = r + i\mu,$

$\quad\quad \lambda_2 = r - i\mu,$

and

$\quad\quad \alpha^{(1)}$ and $\alpha^{(2)}$ are complex conjugates,

then

$$x^{(1)}(t) = (a+ib)e^{(r+i\mu)t}$$

$$= \boxed{(a+ib)e^{rt}(\cos \mu t + i \sin \mu t)} \qquad (6.17)$$

or

$$x^{(1)}(t) = u(t) + iv(t), \quad \text{where}$$

and
$$u(t) = e^{rt}(a \cos \mu t - b \sin \mu t)$$
$$v(t) = e^{rt}(a \sin \mu t + b \cos \mu t)$$

(6.18)

6.9 REPEATED EIGENVALUES

Consider

$$x' = Ax.$$ (6.14)

If $\lambda = \rho$ is repeated twice, then one solution is

$$x^{(1)}(t) = \alpha e^{\rho t}$$

(α satisfies $(A - \rho I)\alpha = 0$).

The second solution is

$$x = \eta t e^{\rho t} + \alpha t e^{\rho t}$$ (6.19)

Substitute (6.19) into (6.14) and then collect like terms, where

$$(A - \rho I)\eta = \alpha$$ (6.20)

If $\lambda = \rho$ is repeated three times:

The first solution is
$$x^{(1)}(t) = \alpha e^{\rho t}$$
The second solution is

$$x^{(2)}(t) = \eta t e^{\rho t} + \alpha t e^{\rho t}$$

The third solution is

$$x^{(3)}(t) = \alpha \frac{t^2}{2!} e^{\rho t} + \eta t e^{\rho t} + \zeta_1 e^{\rho t}$$

For all the solutions, ζ is determined by

$$(A - \rho I)_{\zeta_1} = \eta. \tag{6.21}$$

6.10 NON-HOMOGENEOUS LINEAR SYSTEMS

6.10.1 CONSTANT COEFFICIENT CASE

Consider $x' = Ax + g(t)$. $\tag{6.22}$

Let $x = Ty$ and $y' = Dy + h(t)$ where $h(t) = T^{-1}g(t)$.

D is the diagonal matrix with diagonal entries whose values are the eigenvalues $\lambda_1, \lambda_2, \ldots, \lambda_n$ of A.

In scalar form,

$$y'_j(t) = \lambda_j y_j(t) + h_j(t), \quad j = 1, \ldots, n,$$

and

$$y_j(t) = e^{\lambda_j t} \int e^{-\lambda_j t} h(t) dt + c_j e^{\lambda_j t}, \tag{6.23}$$

where $j = 1, \ldots, n$

6.10.2 VARIABLE COEFFICIENT MATRIX

Consider $x' = P(t)x + g(t)$. $\tag{6.24}$

Let $\psi(t)$ be the solution for the homogeneous case. Use the method of variation of parameters to solve for x:

$$x = \psi(t)u(t),$$

$$\boxed{u(t) = \int \psi^{-1}(t)g(t)\,dt + c} \tag{6.25}$$

with the initial condition $x(t_0) = x^0$,

$$\boxed{x = \phi(t)\,\psi^{-1}(t_0)x^0 + \psi(t)\int \psi^{-1}(t)g(t)\,dt} \tag{6.26}$$

6.11 SYSTEMS OF TOTAL DIFFERENTIAL EQUATIONS

Consider the following pair of total differential equations in 3 variables:

$$P_1dx + Q_1dy + R_1dz = 0 \tag{6.27}$$

and

$$P_2dx + Q_2dy + R_2dz = 0 \tag{6.28}$$

$$f(x,y,z) = c_1 \tag{6.29}$$

and $\qquad g(x,y,z) = c_2 \tag{6.30}$

1. If (6.29) and (6.28) are both integrable,

    then each may be solved separately.

2. If (6.27) is integrable and (6.28) is not,

    Solve (6.29) and use (6.27), (6.28) and (6.29) to eliminate one variable and its differential, and then integrate the result.

3. If neither equation is integrable,

Treat two of the variables, say x and y, as functions of the third. Write the equations in the form

$$\frac{dx}{X} = \frac{dy}{Y} = \frac{dz}{Z},$$

where

$$X = \lambda \begin{vmatrix} Q_1 & R_1 \\ Q_2 & R_2 \end{vmatrix}, \quad Y = \lambda \begin{vmatrix} R_1 & P_1 \\ R_2 & P_2 \end{vmatrix}, \quad Z = \lambda \begin{vmatrix} P_1 & Q_1 \\ P_2 & Q_2 \end{vmatrix}$$

(6.31)

$(\lambda \neq 0)$

an $Ydx = Xdy$, $Xdz = Zdx$, $Zdy = Ydz$

Then apply the previous principles to these equations.

4. If none of the equations are integrable:

Increase the number of possible equation by

$$\frac{dx}{X} = \frac{dy}{Y} = \frac{dz}{Z} = \frac{\ell_1 dx + m_1 dy + n_1 dz}{\ell_1 X + m_1 Y + n_1 Z}$$

$$= \frac{\ell_2 dx + m_2 dy + n_2 dz}{\ell_2 X + m_2 Y + n_2 Z}$$

(6.32)

where $\ell X + mY + nZ \neq 0$, to obtain integrable equations.

CHAPTER 7

THE LAPLACE TRANSFORM

7.1 DEFINITIONS

For the integral transformation

$$F(s) = \int_{\alpha}^{\beta} K(s,t)f(t)dt, \qquad (7.1)$$

K is called the kernel of the transformation. The general idea is to transform a problem for f into a simpler problem for F, to solve this simpler problem, and then to recover the desired function f from its transform F.

The Laplace transform for f, $L\{f(t)\}$, is

$$L\{f(t)\} = F(s) = \int_{0}^{\infty} e^{-st}f(t)dt \qquad (7.2)$$

Conditions for piecewise continuity are:

1. F is continuous within subintervals.

2. $F(t)$ approaches finite limits at either endpoints of these subintervals.

F is said to be of exponential order if

$$e^{-st}|F(t)| < M,$$

where s, t_0 and M are constants, and t_0 and M are positive.

If $f(t)$ is piecewise continuous and of exponential order, then

$$\int_0^\infty e^{-st} f(t) dt$$

exists for $s > \alpha$.

Properties

1. $$\boxed{L\{c_1 f_1(t) + c_2 f_2(t)\} = c_1 L\{f_1(t)\} + c_2 L\{f_2(t)\}}$$ (7.3)

2. $L\{t^n\} = \dfrac{n!}{s^{n+1}}$, n = non-negative integer,
   s = real variable

3. $L\{f'(t)\} = sL\{f(t)\}$

   and

   $L\{\int_0^t f(x) dx\} = \dfrac{1}{s} L\{f(t)\}$

4. $$\boxed{\begin{aligned} L\{f^{(n)}(t)\} = s^n L\{f(t)\} &- s^{n-1} f(o) - s^{n-2} f'(o) \\ &- s^{n-3} f''(o) - \ldots - f^{(n-1)}(o) \end{aligned}}$$

   (7.4)

5. $L\{e^{at} f(t)\} = f(s-a)$, a = constant

6. If $f(s) = L\{f(t)\}$ exists,

   $$L\{t^n f(t)\} = (-1)^n \frac{d^n}{ds^n} [f(s)].$$ (7.5)

7.2 SOLUTIONS OF LINEAR EQUATIONS WITH CONSTANT COEFFICIENTS

Consider the equation

$$a_0 \frac{d^n y}{dt^n} + a_1 \frac{d^{n-1} y}{dt^{n-1}} + \ldots + a_{n-1} \frac{dy}{dt} + a_n y = B(t) \qquad (7.6)$$

and the conditions

$$y(0) = c_0, \quad y'(0) = c_1, \ldots \quad y^{(n-1)}(0) = c_{n-1}. \qquad (7.7)$$

Solution Procedure

1. Take the Laplace transform of both sides of (7.6).

2. Apply the property (7.4):

$$L\left\{\frac{d^n y}{dt^n}\right\} = s^n L\{y(t)\} - s^{n-1} y(0) - s^{n-2} y'(0) - \ldots - y^{(n-1)}(0)$$

$$= s^n L\{y(t)\} - c_0 s^{n-1} - c_1 s^{n-2} - \ldots - c_{n-1},$$

using the conditions (7.7) in the process.

3. Equate the results:

$$[a_0 s^n + a_1 s^{n-1} + \ldots + a_{n-1} s + a_n] y(s)$$

$$- c_0 [a_0 s^{n-1} + a_1 s^{n-2} + \ldots + a_{n-1}] \qquad (7.8)$$

$$- c_1 [a_0 s^{n-2} + a_1 s^{n-3} + \ldots + a_{n-2}]$$

$$- \ldots - c_{n-2} [a_0 s + a_1] - c_{n-1} a_0 = b(s).$$

Equation (7.8) is an algebraic equation in $y(s)$.

4. Solve equation (7.8) to determine $y(s)$.

5. Use the table of transforms to determine the solution

$$y(t) = L^{-1}\{y(s)\}.$$

7.3 SOLUTIONS OF LINEAR SYSTEMS

Consider the system

$$a_1 \frac{dx}{dt} + a_2 \frac{dy}{dt} + a_3 x + a_4 y = B_1(t),$$

$$b_1 \frac{dx}{dt} + b_2 \frac{dy}{dt} - b_3 x + b_4 y = B_2(t) \qquad (7.9)$$

and the conditions

$$X(o) = c_1 \ , \ Y(o) = c_2 . \qquad (7.10)$$

Solution Procedure

1. Let $x(s)$ denote $L\{X(t)\}$ and $y(s)$ denote $L\{Y(t)\}$.

2. Take the Laplace transform of both sides of each equation in (7.9).

3. Apply the property as in section 7-b with conditions of (7.10).

4. Equate the result into a linear algebraic equation in $x(s)$ and $y(s)$.

5. Solve the systems of algebraic equations to determine $x(s)$ and $y(s)$.

6. Use the table of transforms to determine the solutions

$$X(t) = L^{-1}\{x(s)\}$$

and

$$Y(t) = L^{-1}\{y(s)\} .$$

7.4 STEP FUNCTIONS

7.4.1 UNIT STEP FUNCTION

$$u_c(t) = \begin{cases} 0, & t < c \\ 1, & t \geq c, \end{cases} \quad c \geq 0 \qquad (7.11)$$

7.4.2 TRANSLATION OF FUNCTION f

$$y = u_c(t)f(t-c) = \begin{cases} 0, & 0 \leq t < c \\ f(t-c), & t \geq c \end{cases}$$

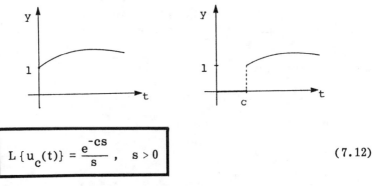

$$\boxed{L\{u_c(t)\} = \frac{e^{-cs}}{s}, \quad s > 0} \qquad (7.12)$$

1. if $F(s) = L\{f(t)\}$ exists for $s > a \geq 0$.

   $$L\{u_c(t)f(t-c)\} = e^{-cs}L\{f(t)\} = e^{-cs}F(s), \quad s > a.$$

2. If $f(t) = L^{-1}\{F(s)\}$, then

   $$u_c(t)f(t-c) = L^{-1}\{e^{-cs}F(s)\}.$$

3. If $F(s) = L\{f(t)\}$ exists for $s > a \geq 0$,

   $$L\{e^{ct}f(t)\} = F(s-c), \quad s > a + c.$$

4. If $f(t) = L^{-1}\{F(s)\}$, then

$e^{ct}f(t) = L^{-1}\{ F(s-c)\}$.

7.5 EQUATIONS WITH DISCONTINUOUS FORCING FUNCTIONS

Consider the equation

$$y'' + p(t)y' + q(t)y = g(t) \qquad\qquad (7.13)$$

where $g(t)$ is piecewise continuous.

If $y = \psi(t)$ is a solution of (7.13), then $\phi''(t)$ will have jump discontinuities at the same points as $g(t)$.

Solution Procedure

1. Write $g(t)$ in unit step function form.

2. Take the Laplace transform.

3. Solve for $y(s)$.

4. Solve for $\phi(t) = L^{-1}\{F(s)\}$.

7.6 IMPULSE FUNCTIONS

1. $$\boxed{I(\tau) = \int_{t_0-\tau}^{t_0+\tau} g(t)dt} \qquad\qquad (7.14)$$

or, since $g(t) = 0$ outside of the interval $(t_0-\tau, t_0+\tau)$,

$$I(t) = \int_{-\infty}^{\infty} g(t)\,dt \qquad (7.15)$$

2. The function δ:

$$\left.\begin{array}{l} \delta(t) = 0, \quad t \neq 0 \\[4mm] \int_{-\infty}^{\infty} \delta(t)\,dt = 1 \end{array}\right\} \quad \text{is called the Dirac "Delta Function"}$$

3. A unit impulse at an arbitrary point $t = t_0$ is

$$\delta(t - t_0): \qquad \delta(t - t_0) = 0, \quad t \neq 0$$

$$\int_{-\infty}^{\infty} \delta(t - t_0)\,dt = 1 \qquad (7.16)$$

4. δ as a limit of the transformation of d_τ is shown by

$$L\{\delta(t - t_0)\} = \lim_{\tau \to 0} L\{d_\tau(t - t_0)\} = e^{-st_0} \qquad (7.17)$$

$$L\{\delta(t)\} = 1. \qquad (7.18)$$

5.
$$\int_{-\infty}^{\infty} \delta(t - t_0)f(t)\,dt = \lim_{\tau \to 0} \int_{-\infty}^{\infty} d_\tau(t - t_0)f(t)\,dt = f(t_0) \qquad (7.19)$$

$$\int_{-\infty}^{\infty} d_\tau(t - t_0)f(t)\,dt = \frac{1}{2\tau} \cdot 2\tau \cdot f(t^*) = f(t^*),$$

$$\text{where } t_0 - \tau < t^* < t_0 + \tau \qquad (7.20)$$

7.7 INVERSE TRANSFORM

Consider a function f.

If the function F is a function whose Laplace transform is the given function f, then F is called the inverse transform of f, and is denoted

$$L^{-1}\{f(s)\} = F(t).$$

Inverse transforms are found by the use of tables.

7.8 CONVOLUTION INTEGRAL

Let $F(t) = L\{f(t)\}$

and $G(t) = L\{g(t)\}.$

Then

$$F(t)*G(t) = \int_0^t F(\tau)G(t-\tau)d\tau \qquad (7.21)$$

is called the convolution of F and G.

Properties

$L\{F*G\} = L\{F\} \, L\{G\}$

$f*g = g*f$

$f*(g_1 + g_2) = f*g_1 + f*g_2$

$(f*g)*h = f*(g*h)$

$f*0 = 0*f = 0.$

7.9 TABLE OF LAPLACE TRANSFORMS

$f(t) = L^{-1}\{F(s)\}$	$F(s) = L\{f(t)\}$
1	$\dfrac{1}{s}, \quad s > 0$
e^{at}	$\dfrac{1}{s-a}, \quad s > a$
t^n, n=positive integer	$\dfrac{n!}{s^{n+1}}, \quad s > 0$
t^p, $p > -1$	$\dfrac{\Gamma(p+1)}{s^{p+1}}, \quad s > 0$
sin at	$\dfrac{a}{s^2+a^2}, \quad s > 0$
cos at	$\dfrac{s}{s^2+a^2}, \quad s > 0$
sinh at	$\dfrac{a}{s^2-a^2}, \quad s > |a|$
cosh at	$\dfrac{s}{s^2-a^2}, \quad s > |a|$
e^{at}sin bt	$\dfrac{b}{(s-a)^2+b^2}, \quad s > a$
e^{at}cos bt	$\dfrac{s-a}{(s-a)^2+b^2}, \quad s > a$
$^n e^{at}$, n=positive integer	$\dfrac{n!}{(s-a)^{n+1}}, \quad s > a$
$u_c(t)$	$\dfrac{e^{-cs}}{s}, \quad s > 0$
$u_c(t)f(t-c)$	$e^{-cs}F(s)$
$e^{ct}f(t)$	$F(s-c)$
$\displaystyle\int_0^t f(t-\tau)g(\tau)d\tau$	$F(s)G(s)$
$f(ct)$	$\dfrac{1}{c} F(\dfrac{s}{c})$
$\delta(t-c)$	e^{-cs}
$f^{(n)}(t)$	$s^n F(s) - s^{n-1}f(0) - \ldots - f^{(n-1)}(0)$
$(-t)^n f(t)$	$F^{(n)}(s)$

THE BEST TEST PREPARATION FOR THE

AP
ADVANCED
PLACEMENT
EXAMINATION

COMPUTER SCIENCE

by Ernest Ackermann, Ph.D. • Mohammed Kamruzzaman, Ph.D. • Jerry Shipman, Ph.D. • John Naymon, Ph.D.

4 Full-Length Exams

➤ Every question based on the current exams
➤ The ONLY test preparation book with detailed explanations to every question
➤ Far more comprehensive than any other test preparation book

Includes a COMPREHENSIVE AP COURSE REVIEW and a Glossary of Computer Science Terms

REA **Research & Education Association**

Available at your local bookstore or order directly from us by sending in coupon below.

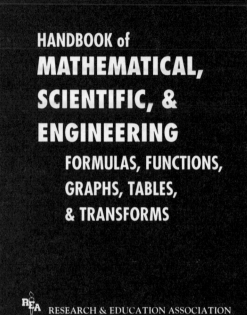

HANDBOOK of
**MATHEMATICAL,
SCIENTIFIC, &
ENGINEERING**
FORMULAS, FUNCTIONS,
GRAPHS, TABLES,
& TRANSFORMS

REA RESEARCH & EDUCATION ASSOCIATION

A particularly useful reference for those in math, science, engineering and other technical fields. Includes the most-often used formulas, tables, transforms, functions, and graphs which are needed as tools in solving problems. The entire field of special functions is also covered. A large amount of scientific data which is often of interest to scientists and engineers has been included.

Available at your local bookstore or order directly from us by sending in coupon below.

REA's **Problem Solvers**

The "PROBLEM SOLVERS" are comprehensive supplemental text-books designed to save time in finding solutions to problems. Each "PROBLEM SOLVER" is the first of its kind ever produced in its field. It is the product of a massive effort to illustrate almost any imaginable problem in exceptional depth, detail, and clarity. Each problem is worked out in detail with a step-by-step solution, and the problems are arranged in order of complexity from elementary to advanced. Each book is fully indexed for locating problems rapidly.

ACCOUNTING
ADVANCED CALCULUS
ALGEBRA & TRIGONOMETRY
AUTOMATIC CONTROL
    SYSTEMS/ROBOTICS
BIOLOGY
BUSINESS, ACCOUNTING, & FINANCE
CALCULUS
CHEMISTRY
COMPLEX VARIABLES
COMPUTER SCIENCE
DIFFERENTIAL EQUATIONS
ECONOMICS
ELECTRICAL MACHINES
ELECTRIC CIRCUITS
ELECTROMAGNETICS
ELECTRONIC COMMUNICATIONS
ELECTRONICS
FINITE & DISCRETE MATH
FLUID MECHANICS/DYNAMICS
GENETICS
GEOMETRY

HEAT TRANSFER
LINEAR ALGEBRA
MACHINE DESIGN
MATHEMATICS for ENGINEERS
MECHANICS
NUMERICAL ANALYSIS
OPERATIONS RESEARCH
OPTICS
ORGANIC CHEMISTRY
PHYSICAL CHEMISTRY
PHYSICS
PRE-CALCULUS
PROBABILITY
PSYCHOLOGY
STATISTICS
STRENGTH OF MATERIALS &
    MECHANICS OF SOLIDS
TECHNICAL DESIGN GRAPHICS
THERMODYNAMICS
TOPOLOGY
TRANSPORT PHENOMENA
VECTOR ANALYSIS

If you would like more information about any of these books,
complete the coupon below and return it to us or visit your local bookstore.

RESEARCH & EDUCATION ASSOCIATION
61 Ethel Road W. • Piscataway, New Jersey 08854
Phone: (732) 819-8880

Please send me more information about your Problem Solver books

Name _____

Address _____

City _____ State _____ Zip _____